T·E·L·L T·A·L·E·S

FOR · OLDER · CHILDREN

CHOSEN·BY·JENNIFER·WILSON
ILLUSTRATED·BY·GRAHAM·COOPER

BLACKIE

CONTENTS

Uninvited Ghosts *by Penelope Lively* 4

The Giant and the Mite *by Eleanor Farjeon* 9

Down River (from *The Cave*) *by Richard Church* 12

Arap Sang and the Cranes *retold by Humphrey Harman* 17

How Loki Outwitted a Giant *retold by Barbara Leonie Picard* 22

Return to Air *by Philippa Pearce* 26

Toothie and Cat *by Gene Kemp* 30

Saviours of the Train (from *The Railway Children*)

by Edith Nesbit 34

INTRODUCTION

A sentence can be as short as one word – 'Go!' How short can a short story be. Some jokes are short stories and they are pretty short. But they still need characters and a beginning, a middle and an end. The end is very important. Do you know people who have you sitting on the edge of your chair wondering what will happen and then forget how the joke ends?

In this collection a few stories are traditional tales first told so long ago that the original teller is not known. Some are by known writers. Edith Nesbit wrote many novels for children and The Railway Children is one that has been made into a film. Several have been television serials. Eleanor Farjeon wrote her own stories as well as rewriting traditional tales. Richard Church wrote many books but only a few for children. In the extract from The Cave spectacles are important. They were important for him: he was so overwhelmed by his new eyes when he put on his first glasses that he lay down on the pavement on the winter afternoon he collected them to see the stars for the first time!

Philippa Pearce, Gene Kemp, and Penelope Lively are prize-winning authors whose new publications are eagerly awaited. They all write both short stories and novels.

Many of the world's greatest authors have written short stories as well as lengthy books and some kept to short stories, enjoying the special challenge of writing them. As in poems there is no space for wasted words. You have to fit an oak into an acorn.

Short stories have interesting shapes. Think of them as journeys. Some go round in a circle ending where they began but with changes on the way. Others climb a mountain with all the excitement of reaching the top in the middle of the adventure, and then come down on a new route the other side. (There is not usually time to explore more than one peak.) A few begin at the peak with the greatest excitement and then come slowly down sorting it all out on the way.

Whichever way the route lies in these stories, it is sure to be worth taking. Have a good journey!

Jennifer Wilson

UNINVITED GHOSTS

Marian and Simon were sent to bed early on the day that the Brown family moved house. By then everyone had lost their temper with everyone else; the cat had been sick on the sitting-room carpet; the dog had run away twice. If you have ever moved you will know what kind of a day it had been. Packing cases and newspaper all over the place ... sandwiches instead of proper meals ... the kettle lost and a wardrobe stuck on the stairs and Mrs Brown's favourite vase broken. There was bread and baked beans for supper, the television wouldn't work and the water wasn't hot so when all was said and done the children didn't object too violently to being packed off to bed. They'd had enough, too. They had one last argument about who was going to sleep by the window, put on their pyjamas, got into bed, switched the lights out ... and it was at that point that the ghost came out of the bottom drawer of the chest of drawers.

It oozed out, a grey cloudy shape about three feet long smelling faintly of woodsmoke, sat down on a chair and began to hum to itself. It looked like a bundle of bedclothes, except that it was not solid: you could see, quite clearly, the cushion on the chair beneath it.

Marian gave a shriek. 'That's a ghost!'

'Oh, be quiet, dear, do,' said the ghost. 'That noise goes right through my head. And it's not nice to call people names.' It took out a ball of wool and some needles and began to knit.

What would you have done? Well, yes—Simon and Marian did just that and I daresay you can imagine what happened. You try telling your mother that you can't get to sleep because there's a ghost sitting in the room clacking its knitting-needles and humming. Mrs Brown said the kind of things she could be expected to say and the ghost continued sitting there knitting and humming and Mrs Brown went out, banging the door and saying threatening things about if there's so much as another word from either of you ....

'She can't see it,' said Marian to Simon.

' 'Course not, dear,' said the ghost. 'It's the kiddies I'm here for. Love kiddies, I do. We're going to be ever such friends.'

'Go away!' yelled Simon. 'This is our house now!'

'No it isn't,' said the ghost smugly. 'Always been here, I have. A hundred years and more. Seen plenty of families come and go, I have. Go to bye-byes now, there's good children.'

The children glared at it and buried themselves under the bedclothes. And, eventually, slept.

The next night it was there again. This time it was smoking a long white pipe and reading a newspaper dated 1842. Beside it was a second grey cloudy shape. 'Hello, dearies,' said the ghost. 'Say how do you do to my Auntie Edna.'

'She can't come here too,' wailed Marian.

'Oh yes she can,' said the ghost. 'Always comes here in August, does Auntie. She likes a change.'

Auntie Edna was even worse, if possible. She sucked peppermint drops that smelled so strong that Mrs Brown, when she came to kiss the children good night, looked suspiciously under their pillows. She also sang hymns in a loud squeaky voice. The children lay there groaning and the ghosts sang and rustled the newspapers and ate peppermints.

The next night there were three of them. 'Meet Uncle Charlie!' said the first ghost. The children groaned.

'And Jip,' said the ghost. 'Here, Jip, good dog – come and say hello to the kiddies, then.' A large grey dog that you could see straight through came out from under the bed, wagging its tail. The cat, who had been curled up beside Marian's feet (it was supposed to sleep in the kitchen, but there are always ways for a resourceful cat to get what it wants), gave a howl and shot on top of the wardrobe, where it sat spitting. The dog lay down in the middle of the rug and set about scratching itself vigorously; evidently it had ghost fleas, too.

Uncle Charlie was unbearable. He had a loud cough that kept going off like a machine-gun and he told the longest most pointless stories the children had ever heard. He said he too loved kiddies and

he knew kiddies loved stories. In the middle of the seventh story the children went to sleep out of sheer boredom.

The following week the ghosts left the bedroom and were to be found all over the house. The children had no peace at all. They'd be quietly doing their homework and all of a sudden Auntie Edna would be breathing down their necks reciting arithmetic tables. The original ghost took to sitting on top of the television with his legs in front of the picture. Uncle Charlie told his stories all through the best programmes and the dog lay permanently at the top of the stairs. The Browns' cat became quite hysterical, refused to eat and went to live on the top shelf of the kitchen dresser.

Something had to be done. Marian and Simon also were beginning to show the effects; their mother decided they looked peaky and bought an appalling sticky brown vitamin medicine from the chemists to strengthen them. 'It's the ghosts!' wailed the children. 'We don't need vitamins!' Their mother said severely that she didn't want to hear another word of this silly nonsense about ghosts. Auntie Edna, who was sitting smirking on the other side of the kitchen table at that very moment, nodded vigorously and took out a packet of humbugs which she sucked noisily.

'We've got to get them to go and live somewhere else,' said Marian. But where, that was the problem, and how? It was then that they had a bright idea. On Sunday the Browns were all going to see their uncle who was rather rich and lived alone in a big house with thick carpets everywhere and empty rooms and the biggest colour television you ever saw. Plenty of room for ghosts.

They were very cunning. They suggested to the ghosts that they might like a drive in the country. The ghosts said at first that they were quite comfortalble where they were, thank you, and they didn't fancy these new-fangled motor-cars, not at their time of life. But then Auntie Edna remembered that she liked looking at the pretty flowers and the trees and finally they agreed to give it a try. They sat in a row on the back shelf of the car. Mrs Brown kept asking why there was such a strong smell of peppermint and Mr Brown kept roaring at Simon and Marian to keep still while he was driving. The fact was that the ghosts were shoving them; it was like being nudged by three cold damp flannels. And the ghost dog, who had come along too of course, was car-sick.

When they got to Uncle Dick's the ghosts came in and had a look round. They liked the expensive carpets and the enormous television. They slid in and out of the wardrobes and walked through the doors and the walls and sent Uncle Dick's budgerigars into a decline from which they have never recovered. Nice place, they said, nice and comfy.

'Why not stay here?' said Simon, in an offhand tone.

'Couldn't do that,' said the ghosts firmly. 'No kiddies. Dull. We like a place with a bit of life to it.' And they piled back into the car and sang hymns all the way home to the Browns' house. They also ate toast. There were real toast-crumbs on the floor and the children got the blame.

Simon and Marian were in despair. The ruder they were to the ghosts the more the ghosts liked it. 'Cheeky!' they said indulgently. 'What a cheeky little pair of kiddies! There now . . . come and give uncle a kiss.' The children weren't even safe in the bath. One or other of the ghosts would come and sit on the taps and talk to them. Uncle Charlie had produced a mouth organ and played the same tune over and over again; it was quite excruciating. The children went around with their hands over their ears. Mrs Brown took them to the doctor to find out if there was something wrong with their hearing. The children knew better than to say anything to the doctor about the ghosts. It was pointless saying anything to anyone.

I don't know what would have happened if Mrs Brown hadn't happened to make friends with Mrs Walker from down the road. Mrs Walker had twin babies, and one day she brought the babies along for tea.

Now one baby is bad enough. Two babies are trouble in a big way. These babies created pandemonium. When they weren't both howling they were crawling around the floor pulling the tablecloths off the tables or hitting their heads on the chairs and hauling the books out of the bookcases. They threw their food all over the kitchen and flung cups of milk on the floor. Their mother mopped up after them and every time she tried to have a conversation with

7

Mrs Brown the babies bawled in chorus so that no one could hear a word.

In the middle of this the ghosts appeared. One baby was yelling its head off and the other was glueing pieces of chewed up bread onto the front of the television. The ghosts swooped down on them with happy cries. 'Oh!' they trilled. 'Bless their little hearts then, diddums, give auntie a smile then.' And the babies stopped in mid-howl and gazed at the ghosts. The ghosts cooed at the babies and the babies cooed at the ghosts. The ghosts chattered to the babies and sang them songs and the babies chattered back and were as good as gold for the next hour and their mother had the first proper conversation she'd had in weeks. When they went the ghosts stood in a row at the window, waving.

Simon and Marian knew when to seize an opportunity. That evening they had a talk with the ghosts. At first the ghosts raised objections. They didn't fancy the idea of moving, they said; you got set in your ways, at their age; Auntie Edna reckoned a strange house would be the death of her.

The children talked about the babies, relentlessly.

And the next day they led the ghosts down the road, followed by the ghost dog, and into the Walkers' house. Mrs Walker doesn't know to this day why the babies who had been screaming for the last half hour suddenly stopped and broke into great smiles. And she has never understood why, from that day forth, the babies became the most tranquil, quiet, amiable babies in the area. The ghosts kept the babies amused from morning to night. The babies thrived; the ghosts were happy; the ghost dog, who was actually a bitch, settled down so well that she had puppies which is one of the most surprising aspects of the whole business. The Brown children heaved a sigh of relief and got back to normal life. The babies, though, I have to tell you, grew up somewhat peculiar.

Penelope Lively

THE GIANT AND THE MITE

There was once a Giant who was too big to be seen. As he walked about, the space between his legs was so great that nobody could see as far as from one side to the other, and his head was so high in the sky that nobody's eyes were strong enough to see the top of him. Not being able to take him in all at once, nobody therefore knew that the Giant existed.

Sometimes men felt his footsteps shake the earth, and then they said:

'There has been another earthquake.'

And sometimes they felt his shadow pass over them, and they said:

'What a dark day it is!'

And sometimes, when he stooped down to scratch his leg, they felt him breathe, and said:

'Phew! what a wind!'

And that was as much as they knew about him.

But little as it was, it was more than he knew about them; for in spite of his size the Giant had no mind. His legs could walk, and his lungs could breathe, but his brain couldn't think. Of this he had no suspicion, and was quite contented to go on walking about all day, or to stop still and sleep all night; and when he was hungry, he opened his mouth and ate up a star or two, pulling them off the sky with his lips as you might pull cherries off a tree.

At the same time, there was a Mite who was too small to be seen. He was so small that even the ants couldn't see him, and perhaps that was lucky; for if they had done so, they might have gobbled him up. A grain of sand was like a mountain to him, and it would have taken him longer than his whole life to walk across a sixpence. So you can fancy what a tiny bit he moved day by day from the spot where he was born. But he himself never knew this; a tiny way to him was as much as a hundred miles to you, and if his body did not go far, his mind went a great way. For the Mite had a mind, and could think; he was indeed almost all Mind, and his thoughts were as big as the Giant, who couldn't think at all.

Now up in the sky and under the earth sat the two Angels who can see all. Nothing is too big or too small for them, or too far away, or too long ago. One day the Angel in the Sky said to the Angel under the Earth:

'What have you seen today?'

'I have seen a Giant,' said the Angel under the Earth, 'who is so strong that his strength could break the world in two.'

'I know him well,' said the Angel in the Sky, 'and one of these days he is quite likely to break the world in two without thinking.'

'And what have you seen today?' asked the Angel under the Earth.

'I have seen a Mite,' said the Angel in the Sky, 'whose mind is so powerful that it could make a new world altogether, if it had the strength to do it with.'

'I've seen him often,' said the Angel under the Earth, 'thinking and thinking of worlds that he will never make.'

It happened one day that the Giant lay down to sleep, with the tip of his right forefinger covering the acre of earth that happened to contain the Mite. The following morning, in helping himself up, he carried away the acre of earth under his fingernail, and the Mite with it. A short while after he happened to scratch his ear, and in doing so he dislodged from under his nail the field in which the Mite was hidden, which to the Giant was but a speck of dirt. In the course of time this speck worked its way through the Giant's ear until it reached his brain. As soon as this happened a marvellous change took place.

For the Giant, who had never had a thought in all his life, suddenly began to think; and he did not know that the Mite was thinking for him. And the Mite, who had never had any strength of his own, suddenly felt that he had the power to make worlds and break them; and he did not know that his strength was in the body of the Giant. Each seemed to himself, not two creatures, but one. And the thoughts of the Mite made the Giant long to do all sorts of things, and the strength of the Giant made the Mite able to carry out his thoughts.

Now terrible things began to happen in the world, and all around it. Between them, the Giant and the Mite tore up mountains and let the sea run in, and they scooped up the rivers and flung them into the clouds, and they moved the moons and stars all about the sky, arranging them in different patterns every night, and they took the

10

wind between thumb and finger, held it up to the Sun, and blew the Sun out. Then they poked a hole with a finger into the middle of the earth, fetched up a handful of fire, and lit the Sun up again. At last it began to look, not so much as though the world would come to an end, as that it would never get on to its end at all, but go backwards or forwards, or up or down, or round and round, or inside out, just as the Mite and the Giant might fancy at any moment.

Then the Angel in the Sky said to the Angel under the Earth:

'This will never do. Between them they will mix up earth and heaven till nobody knows which is which.'

The Angel under the Earth replied, 'There's only one thing for it; we must reduce them to the size of a man.'

'Ah, but,' said the Angel in the Sky, 'size is just an idea, like everything else. We must not only make them equal in size to men, we must also make them look at one another for a moment, so that they shall know forever after they are not one thing but two.'

In a twinkling the thing was done. The body of the Giant shrank till it became that of a splendid man in full strength, and the Mite looked out from his eyes and saw the form he dwelt in, of which he had never before been aware. At the same moment the Giant was given the power to look inside himself, and there he beheld the Mite.

'Hullo!' said the Giant.

'Hello!' said the Mite.

'What are *you* doing in there?' said the Giant.

'I've just looked in,' said the Mite.

'Well, stay a bit,' said the Giant, 'and between us we might manage to do something.'

'No harm trying,' said the Mite.

So they agreed upon it, and the Angel under the Earth and the Angel in the Sky smiled up and down at each other with just the same sort of smile.

From that day forth, the Giant and the Mite did very little; for each wanted to do such different things that they seldom agreed.

Only once in a great while they forgot they were two and not one, and wanted to do the same thing. When that happened, the Angels held their breath until the Giant and the Mite remembered themselves again, and the danger was past.

Eleanor Farjeon

DOWN RIVER

These flesh-coloured brackets attracted the boys' attention at once, and both flashed their torches on the sinister objects. From moment to moment a drop of water, tossed from the cauldron below, alighted on the leathery surface of the fungi and was at once absorbed, leaving a thumb mark of stain which instantly followed the water drop into oblivion. Thus, the surface of these brackets was constantly in colour-motion, like the keyboard of a piano when the player's fingers are pressing down the ivories, making momentary shadows on the white surface. Added to that play of colour, the substance of the fungi trembled somewhat, as though shivering within its own stillness. All this gave it the appearance of being alive. The little brackets might have been half-formed human hands, born from the rock and trembling under the impulse of some remote fear.

How long Lightning and John had been watching these objects, they could not tell, so strong was the spell. They were recalled to reality, however, by the spray which had gathered on John's spectacles. The moment came when he could see nothing except a blur of broken light, and he had to take off his spectacles in order to wipe them. He could not grope about for his beloved piece of wash leather, so he removed his hand from Lightning's shoulders in order to take his handkerchief from his trousers pocket. This action, unfortunately, caused Lightning to turn around sharply to see what

John was doing. The small boy always moved and thought in that way, with a bird-like rather than a human habit of mind and body. His abrupt movement caused John to jerk the arm and drop the spectacles. As they left his hand, one of the ear-pieces caught in his finger and caused the spectacles to be thrown out, away from the rock, into the centre of the waterfall. The sudden clearing of his sight caused John to see distinctly and thus to overcome his disability. Both he and Lightning, in dismay, watched the spectacles alight on the cauldron, to be flung up on the other side of the pool without encountering anything hard. Then they gradually settled down to the bed of the stream and could be seen, trembling and wavering, on the bottom.

Before John could realize what had happened, Lightning had set his torch down on his haversack, slipped off his clothes and plunged into the centre of the pool.

John was terrified. The seething mass of water at the bottom of the fall took hold of the small white body of his companion, quarrelling over it like a nest of snakes over a captured bird. John picked up the second torch and directed both beams on to the water. He saw Lightning sucked under and thrown up again, and he tried to shout to him but was unable to make a sound from his paralysed throat. The force of the water, however, pushed Lightning out of the deep pool, and at the same moment, the boy struck out and swirled down stream for several yards, after which he regained his depth and touched the right bank. Here he was able to stand up and turn to face John, but he had to crouch forward to withstand the rush of the stream. John could see him shivering. Above the turmoil of the fall, his voice rose, trembling like a reed:

'It's mighty cold, John, but I can make my way back.'

He proceeded to do so, battling against the river by the help of the rocky bosses and ledges along the bank, which he gripped, hand over hand, thus being able to pull himself along against the current.

John, meanwhile, focused the beams of both torches on to the pair of spectacles lying safely on the river bed.

'There they are,' he cried, no longer alarmed for Lightning's safety.

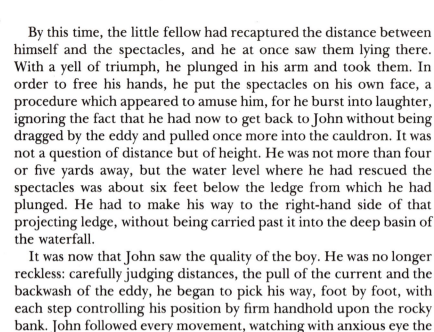

By this time, the little fellow had recaptured the distance between himself and the spectacles, and he at once saw them lying there. With a yell of triumph, he plunged in his arm and took them. In order to free his hands, he put the spectacles on his own face, a procedure which appeared to amuse him, for he burst into laughter, ignoring the fact that he had now to get back to John without being dragged by the eddy and pulled once more into the cauldron. It was not a question of distance but of height. He was not more than four or five yards away, but the water level where he had rescued the spectacles was about six feet below the ledge from which he had plunged. He had to make his way to the right-hand side of that projecting ledge, without being carried past it into the deep basin of the waterfall.

It was now that John saw the quality of the boy. He was no longer reckless: carefully judging distances, the pull of the current and the backwash of the eddy, he began to pick his way, foot by foot, with each step controlling his position by firm handhold upon the rocky bank. John followed every movement, watching with anxious eye the battle of muscle and brain against the blind force of the water. It was a beautiful scene; the toss and tumble of the fall, clothed in its own spray, the sombre indifference of the rocks, the fish-like fragility of Lightning's body, more water-sprite than human.

But John was in no mood to enjoy this purely as a picture. Indeed, he was cold with the misery of it. Could it be possible that the tiny white object, creeping along the side of the tunnel, could possibly endure for more than a few minutes? John could already foresee that as soon as Lightning relaxed his hold in order to reach up towards the ledge, the current would seize him from the waist downward, pull him back into the cauldron and drown him.

Without further reflection, he lay flat on the ledge and reached down with his stick, through the crook of which he had slipped the rope so that the noose hung out a couple of feet over the water. He had to do this with one hand while with the other he held the torch to direct Lightning to the lifeline. The boy gradually approached, and John strained himself downward reaching as far as possible. Both made an extra effort to bridge the gap. Grunting as he did so, John gave a flick to the rope by lifting the stick a little. At the same moment, Lightning stood upright, grabbed at the noose and missed it. The movement put him at the mercy of the water, and he was thrown off his balance. Down he went, and began to swirl around towards the head of the ledge. Beyond it lay the great pool and the tumult of waters under the fall.

Then a miracle happened; or what might well be called a miracle. It was really an effort of will, but probably that is the same thing, for it means a triumph over circumstances. With instant speed, John changed over the stick and the torch, thus having the stick in his left hand. At the same time, he propelled his body leftward to the extreme edge of the rocky pier, while he shook the stick freely and was thus able to pay out a couple of extra feet of rope. The noose hit the water and was instantly worried by it, shaking and tugging at the stick in John's hand. But he kept control, and the rope lay on the water directly in the path where Lightning was being dragged back. John felt him seize it and the stick was almost dragged out of his hand. Instinctively, he put down the torch on the rock beside him and the beam of light was thus thrown, ineffectively, across the wall of the tunnel, leaving the waterfall in darkness. It also left the struggling boy in darkness, but John could feel him securely on the end of the rope.

'Hold on!' he shouted, and with that he drew in the stick and seized the rope with both hands. The stick was now lying under him and was in his way. He wriggled back a little, and extricated it, pushing it to one side of his body. He was now firmly set on the ledge, with one foot anchored in a cleft of rock. He had the rope under him and could play it with both hands. The trouble was that he could not see because the pool beneath was in darkness, and, also, he was without his spectacles. Happily he was able to leave go

with the right hand for a moment, grab the torch, and so fix it that once more its beam lit the scene of action. He saw the misty form of Lightning hanging on the end of the rope, his head above water; the situation seemed to last for hours, but, in fact, only a few moments passed before Lightning was able by the help of the rope to pull himself back to the wall and to regain his footing.

He was now safely anchored with the rope in one hand and a firm ledge of rock under the other. John flashed a torch to try to find a foothold for Lightning to lift himself out of the water and climb to the ledge. The light fell on an upturned face lit by a mischievous grin and the flashing lenses of the spectacles.

'They're quite safe,' cried the shrill voice.

'You're an imbecile,' retorted John, trying to be more savage than he felt. 'I've now got to get you up here and probably bring flowers to the funeral when you've died of pneumonia.'

'Rot,' cried Lightning. 'If you'd been fighting against the stream, you'd be as hot as I am.'

'All the more reason to get you out of it,' said John, and with that, he let down the other end of the rope and instructed Lightning to tie it loosely around his waist. Thus secured, the boy was now able to reach the ledge, and within a few minutes his skin was glowing with warmth after he had rubbed himself down with his own shirt.

John, once more in possession of his spectacles, felt it his duty still to be severe and to disguise his gratitude and admiration.

'You know,' he said, 'it's all very well, but you must realize that you are responsible to other people for your own safety.'

This solemn remark caused Lightning to lift up his voice and crow like a cock, a reply that destroyed all possibilities of seriousness. Suddenly, in that strange scene above the waterfall, with the appalling flood slipping away into the darkness of the tunnel beyond, a peal of laughter rose from the two urchins who had yet to find a way to save themselves from destruction.

Richard Church
an extract from
The Cave

ARAP SANG AND THE CRANES

The people of Africa believe that before you give anything to anyone you should first carefully think out what your gift will mean to him. They are often shocked at the way white men give things, anything, tractors and trousers, guns and radios, showering them down on people's heads with no kind of thought about what they will *mean* to the people who get the presents. Like being given a camera when you can't afford to buy films. That's worse than not having a camera.

A gift is a great responsibility to the giver, they say, and after they have said that they may tell you the story of Arap Sang and the Cranes.

Arap Sang was a great chief and more than half a god, for in the days when he lived great chiefs were always a little mixed up with the gods. One day he was walking on the plain admiring the cattle.

It was hot. The rains had not yet come; the ground was almost bare of grass and as hard as stone; the thorn trees gave no shade, for they were just made of long spines and thin twigs and tiny leaves, and the sun went straight through them.

It was hot. Only the black ants didn't feel it and they would be happy in a furnace.

Arap Sang was getting old and the sun beat down on his bald head (he was sensitive about this and didn't like it mentioned) and he thought: 'I'm feeling things more than I used.'

And then he came across a vulture sitting in the crotch of a tree, his wings hanging down and his eyes on the look-out.

'Vulture,' said Arap Sang, 'I'm hot and the sun is making my head ache. You have there a fine pair of broad wings. I'd be most grateful if you'd spread them out and let an old man enjoy a patch of shade.'

'Why?' croaked Vulture. He had indigestion. Vultures usually have indigestion, it's the things they eat.

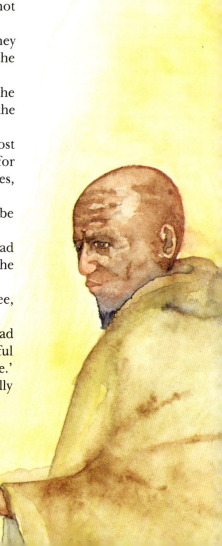

'Why?' said Arap Sang mildly. 'Now that's a question to which I'm not certain that I've got the answer. Why? Why, I suppose, because I ask you. Because I'm an old man and entitled to a little assistance and respect. Because it wouldn't be much trouble to you. Because it's pleasant and good to help people.'

'Bah!' said Vulture.

'What's that?'

'Oh, go home, Baldy, and stop bothering people, it's hot.'

Arap Sang straightened himself up and his eyes flashed. He wasn't half a god for nothing and when he was angry he could be rather a terrible old person. And he was very angry now. It was that remark about his lack of hair.

The really terrifying thing was that when he spoke he didn't shout. He spoke quietly and the words were clear and cold and hard. And all separate like hailstones.

'Vulture,' he said, 'you're cruel and you're selfish. I shan't forget what you've said and you won't either. NOW GET OUT!'

Arap Sang was so impressive that Vulture got up awkwardly and flapped off.

'Silly old fool,' he said, uncomfortably.

Presently he met an acquaintance of his (vultures don't have friends, they just have acquaintances) and they perched together on the same bough. Vulture took a close look at his companion and then another and what he saw was so funny that it cheered him up.

'He, he!' he giggled. 'What's happened to you? Met with an accident? You're bald.'

The other vulture looked sour, but at the same time you felt he might be pleased about something.

'That's good, coming from you,' he said. 'What have you been up to? You haven't got a feather on you above the shoulders.'

Then they both felt their heads with consternation. It was quite

true. They were bald, both of them, and so was every other vulture, the whole family, right down to this very day.

Which goes to show that if you can't be ordinarily pleasant to people at least it's not wise to go insulting great chiefs who are half gods.

I said that he was rather a terrible old person.

Arap Sang walked on. He was feeling shaky. Losing his temper always upset him afterwards and doing the sort of magic that makes every vulture in the world bald in the wink of an eye, takes it out of you if you aren't as young as you used to be.

And he did want a bit of shade.

Presently he met an elephant. Elephant was panting across the plain in a tearing hurry and was most reluctant to stop when Arap Sang called to him.

'Elephant,' said Arap Sang weakly, 'I'm tired and I'm dizzy. I want to get to the forest and into a bit of shade but it's a long way.'

'It is hot, isn't it?' said Elephant. 'I'm off to the forest myself.'

'Would you spread out your great ears and let me walk along under them?' asked Arap Sang.

'I'm sorry,' said Elephant, 'but you'd make my journey so slow. I must get to the forest. I've got the most terrible headache.'

'Well, I've got a headache too,' protested the old man.

'I'm sure you have,' said Elephant, 'and no one could be sorrier about that than I am. Is it a very big headache?'

'Shocking big,' said Arap Sang.

'There now,' said Elephant. 'Consider how big I am compared to you and what the size of my headache must be.'

That's elephants all over, always so logical. Arap Sang felt that there was something wrong with this argument but he couldn't just see where. Also he had become a little uncomfortable about all those bald vultures and he didn't want to lose his temper with

19

anyone else. You have to be careful what you do when you're half a god. It's so dreadfully final.

'Oh, all right,' he muttered.

'Knew you'd see it that way,' said Elephant. 'It's just what I was saying about you the other day. You can always rely on Arap Sang, I said, to behave reasonably. Well, good-bye and good luck.'

And he hurried off in the direction of the distant forest and was soon out of sight.

Poor Arap Sang was now feeling very ill indeed. He sat on the ground and he thought to himself: 'I can't go another step unless I get some shade and if I don't get some soon I'm done for.'

And there he was found by a flock of cranes.

They came dancing through the white grass, stamping their long delicate legs so that the insects flew up in alarm and were at once snapped up in the cranes' beaks. They gathered round Arap Sang sitting on the ground, and he looked so old and distressed that they hopped up and down with embarrassment, first on one leg then the other. 'Korong! Korong!' they called softly and this happens to be their name as well.

'Good birds,' whispered Arap Sang, 'you must help me. If I don't reach shade soon I'll die. Help me to the forest.'

'But of course,' said the cranes, and they spread their great handsome black and white wings to shade him and helped him to his feet, and together, slowly, they all crossed the plain into the trees.

Then Arap Sang sat in the shade of a fine cotton tree and felt very much better. The birds gathered round him and he looked at them and thought that he had never seen more beautiful creatures in the whole world.

'And kind. Kind as well as beautiful,' he muttered. 'The two don't always go together. I must reward them.'

'I shan't forget your kindness,' he said, 'and I'll see that no one else does. Now I want each one of you to come here.'

Then the cranes came one after another and bowed before him and Arap Sang stretched out his kindly old hand and gently touched each beautiful sleek head. And where he did this a golden crown appeared and after the birds had gravely bowed their thanks they all flew off to the lake, their new crowns glittering in the evening sun.

Arap Sang felt quite recovered. He was very pleased with his gift to the cranes.

Two months later a crane dragged himself to the door of Arap Sang's house. It was a pitiful sight, thin with hunger, feathers broken and muddy from hiding in the reeds, eyes red with lack of sleep.

Arap Sang exclaimed in pity and horror.

'Great Chief,' said the crane, 'we beg you to take back your gift. If you don't there'll soon be not one crane left alive, for we are hunted day and night for the sake of our golden crowns.'

Arap Sang listened and nodded his head in sorrow.

'I'm old and I'm foolish,' he said, 'and I harm my friends. I had forgotten that men also were greedy and selfish and that they'll do anything for gold. Let me undo the wrong I have done by giving without thought. I'll make one more magic but that'll be the last.'

Then he took their golden crowns and in their place he put a wonderful halo of feathers which they have until this day.

But they are still called Crowned Cranes.

retold by
Humphrey Harman

HOW LOKI OUTWITTED A GIANT

A certain peasant and his wife lived with their young son in a little house nearby the sea. The man was greatly fond of playing chess, and frequent practice with his neighbours on the long winter evenings had brought him much skill at the game. One day a giant came to the cottage and demanded that the peasant should play chess with him. Glad to match himself with an opponent whom he had not tried before, the man consented. 'But for what stakes do we play?' he asked, for he much enjoyed winning a coin or two or a measure of wheat from his neighbours.

'Whichever of us wins may ask the other for what he will of his possessions,' replied the giant promptly.

And the man thought to himself, 'I am poor, there is but little among my possessions that a giant could covet, yet will he own much that would be of use to me, should the victory be mine.' And he agreed to the stakes, and they sat down to play together.

The game was a long one, and went on well into the evening, but at last the giant won. 'Now must you give to me out of all that you own that which I shall choose for myself,' he said.

'Choose and welcome,' said the peasant. 'It was a good game and I would not have missed it.'

'Give me your son,' said the giant. 'He is all I want of your possesssions.'

The unfortunate man heard the words with horror; but in vain he and his wife implored the giant to take all else they owned and leave them their only child, for the giant did no more than laugh at their pleading. Yet at last, to their entreaties, he replied, 'I will leave you the boy for one night longer and tomorrow I shall come for him. And more, if tomorrow you have hidden him so well that I cannot find him, I will renounce my claim and you may keep your son.' And with that he went away.

Weeping, the peasant and his wife wondered where they might hide the child, but they could think of no place where the giant would not look for him. Far on into the night they thought despairingly, and at last the woman said, 'Let us pray to Odin, he may hear us and come to our aid.'

So they prayed to Odin, and after a time there came a great knocking in the darkness on the cottage door. 'It is the giant returned,' said the woman fearfully. But her husband replied, 'It is not yet dawn, he will not come in the night.' And he went bravely to the door and opened it.

Outside stood a stranger in a grey cloak with a wide-brimmed hat, none other than Odin himself. 'I have heard your prayers,' he said. 'Give me your son and I will hide him for you, and maybe the giant will not find him when he comes in the morning.'

Gratefully the peasant and his wife gave the child to Odin and Odin changed him into a grain of wheat and hid the grain in an ear growing in a wheatfield close by.

In the morning the giant came and looked once around the cottage. 'You have not hidden him here,' he said, and went outside. He looked all about him, and then, having some strange knowledge, he went straight to the wheatfield, while the peasant and his wife watched with troubled eyes. 'Give me a sickle,' demanded the giant, and the man dared not refuse him.

Rapidly the giant cut the wheat, casting aside each armful save one, and then he flung down the sickle and picked out a single ear of wheat from among the rest he held. Then he plucked off, one by one, each grain, until he held the very one which was the boy. The peasant and his wife wrung their hands in despair; but Odin, taking pity on them once again, blew like a puff of wind and tossed the grain of wheat out of the giant's grasp and back to the man and his wife, where it became once more the boy. 'I have done what I can for you,' said Odin. 'Now must you help yourselves.'

The giant strode over to the cottage. 'That was good,' he said, 'but it was not good enough. You will have to outwit me more cleverly than that, if you wish to keep your son. Tomorrow I shall come again to find where you have hidden him.'

All that night the peasant and his wife wondered what they should do, now that Odin could help them no longer; and at last they

prayed to Hönir, the bright god, Odin's brother. And just before dawn, when the woman opened the door of the cottage to see if it was yet day, there outside stood Hönir, like a ray of light. 'Give me your son,' he said, 'and I will hide him for you, and maybe the giant will not find him when he comes.'

Gratefully they gave him the boy; and Hönir turned him into a tiny feather and hid him on the breast of a swan which swam on a stream close by.

In the morning the giant came and looked once around the cottage. 'You have not hidden him here,' he said, and went outside. He looked all about him, and then, having some strange knowledge, he went straightway to the stream and snatched up the swan and tore off its head. Then he plucked off its feathers one by one, while the peasant and his wife watched him with dismay. At last the giant held in his hands one fluff of white down which was the boy, and the father and the mother wrung their hands in despair.

But Hönir took pity on them and blew like a puff of wind and blew the feather into the cottage where it became the boy again. 'I have done what I can for you,' said Hönir. 'Now must you help yourselves.'

The giant came to the peasant and said, 'That too was good, but it was not good enough. Tomorrow I shall come again to find where you have hidden him.'

Once more the man and his wife wondered all night what they might do to save their son, now that Odin and Hönir could not help them; and towards dawn they were still sitting over the ashes of their fire, their faces white and drawn. The man shivered. 'The fire is dying,' he said. And glad to do something other than think, the woman raked the ashes and laid wood on them. Suddenly she said, 'There is yet Loki.'

'Why should Loki help us?' asked her husband.

'We can but pray to him,' she said.

So they prayed to Loki that he would save their son, and waited in the grey darkness for an answer. And suddenly the wood caught fire and blazed up, and in the light of the flames, there stood Loki in the room. 'Give me your son,' he said, 'and I will hide him for you, and maybe the giant will not find him when he comes.'

They gave the child to Loki, who changed him into the tiny egg of a fish, and went from the cottage down to the sea and hid the egg in the roe of a flounder that swam far from the shore.

When the giant came he looked once around the cottage and said, 'He is not here, he is outside.' And he went out and looked about him. Then, having some strange knowledge, he hurried off to fetch his boat and dragged it down to the shore, while the peasant and his wife watched him with terror. But as the giant climbed aboard, Loki came up to him. 'Take me fishing with you,' he demanded.

'Willingly,' said the giant, and they put out to sea together.

In the middle of the ocean the giant baited his hook and fished; but each fish that he caught he flung overboard again, until he caught a certain flounder, and placing it carefully in the bottom of the boat, he rowed once more for the shore.

On the beach he took out his knife and cut the fish open to take out the roe. Splitting the roe, he looked each egg over until he held the one which was the boy between his finger and his thumb. 'This time have I caught you,' he laughed.

'What have you there?' asked Loki.

'No more than a flounder's egg,' said the giant.

'No one would take such care of a flounder's egg,' scoffed Loki. 'Show it to me.'

The giant moved aside his thumb so that Loki could see he spoke the truth, and in that instant Loki snatched the egg and it became once more the child. 'Go, hide yourself in your father's boathouse,' said Loki. And the terrified boy ran across the beach to the little boathouse, and going in, shut the door behind him.

The giant instantly started off in pursuit, flung open the boathouse door and thrust his head inside, shouting to the boy to come out. But as Loki had thought he would, the giant forgot how small the boathouse was, and he struck his head on a beam and fell down senseless. Loki immediately ran up and killed the giant with his own fishing knife and the boy was saved.

And ever after, the grateful peasant and his wife considered Loki the greatest of all the gods, for he alone had not said to them, 'I have done what I can. Now must you help yourselves,' but had stayed to see his trick through to the end.

retold by
Barbara Leonie Picard

RETURN TO AIR

The Ponds are very big, so that at one end people bathe and at the other end they fish. Old chaps with bald heads sit on folding stools and fish with rods and lines, and little kids squeeze through the railings and wade out into the water to fish with nets. But the water's much deeper at our end of the Pond, and that's where we bathe. You're not allowed to bathe there unless you can swim; but I've always been able to swim. They used to say that was because fat floats - well, I don't mind. They call me Sausage.

Only, I don't dive – not from any diving-board, thank you. I have to take my glasses off to go into the water, and I can't see without them, and I'm just not going to dive, even from the lowest diving-board, and that's that, and they stopped nagging about it long ago.

Then, this summer, they were all on to me to learn duck-diving. You're swimming on the surface of the water and suddenly you up-end yourself just like a duck and dive down deep into the water, and perhaps you swim about a bit under-water, and then come up again. I daresay ducks begin doing it soon after they're born. It's different for them.

So I was learning to duck-dive - to swim down to the bottom of the Ponds, and pick up a brick they'd thrown in, and bring it up again. You practise that in case you have to rescue anyone from drowning – say, they'd sunk for the third time and gone to the bottom. Of course, they'd be bigger and heavier than a brick, but I suppose you have to begin with bricks and work up gradually to people.

The swimming-instructor said, 'Sausage, I'm going to throw the brick in –' It was a brick with a bit of old white flannel round it, to make it show up under-water. '– Sausage, I'm going to throw it in, and you go *after* it – go *after* it, Sausage, and get it before it reaches the bottom and settles in the mud, or you'll never get it.'

He'd made everyone come out of the water to give me a chance, and they were standing watching. I could see them blurred along the bank, and I could hear them talking and laughing; but there wasn't a sound in the water except me just treading water gently, waiting. And then I saw the brick go over my head as the instructor threw it, and there was a splash as it went into the water ahead of me; and I thought: I can't do it – my legs won't upend this time – they feel just flabby – they'll float, but they won't upend – they can't upend – it's different for ducks... But while I was thinking all that, I'd taken a deep breath, and then my head really went down and my legs went up into the air – I could feel them there, just air around them, and then there was water round them, because I was going down into the water, after all. Right down into the water; straight down...

At first my eyes were shut, although I didn't know I'd shut them. When I did realize, I forced my eyelids up against the water to see. Because, although I can't see much without my glasses, as I've said, I don't believe anyone could see much under-water in those Ponds; so I could see as much as anyone.

The water was like a thick greeny-brown lemonade, with wispy little things moving very slowly about in it – or perhaps they were just movements of the water, not things at all; I couldn't tell. The brick had a few seconds' start of me, of course, but I could still see a whitish glimmer that must be the flannel round it: it was ahead of me, fading away into the lower water, as I moved after it.

The funny thing about swimming under-water is its being so still and quiet and shady down there, after all the air and sunlight and splashing and shouting just up above. I was shut right in by the quiet, greeny-brown water, just me alone with the brick ahead of me, both of us making towards the bottom.

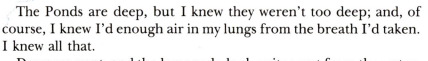

The Ponds are deep, but I knew they weren't too deep; and, of course, I knew I'd enough air in my lungs from the breath I'd taken. I knew all that.

Down we went, and the lemonade-look quite went from the water, and it became just a dark blackish-brown, and you'd wonder you could see anything at all. Especially as the bit of white flannel seemed to have come off the brick by the time it reached the bottom and I'd caught up with it. The brick looked different down there, anyway, and it had already settled right into the mud – there was only one corner left sticking up. I dug into the mud with my fingers and got hold of the thing, and then I didn't think of anything except getting up again with it into the air. Touching the bottom like that had stirred up the mud, so that I began going up through a thick cloud of it. I let myself go up – they say fat floats, you know – but I was shooting myself upwards, too. I was in a hurry.

The funny thing was, I only began to be afraid when I was going back. I suddenly thought: perhaps I've swum under-water much too far – perhaps I'll come up at the far end of the Ponds among all the fishermen and foul their lines and perhaps get a fish-hook caught in the flesh of my cheek. And all the time I was going up quite quickly and the water was changing from brown-black to green-brown and then to bright lemonade. I could almost see the sun shining through the water, I was so near the surface. It wasn't until then that I felt really frightened: I thought I was moving much too slowly and I'd never reach the air again in time.

Never the air again...

Then suddenly I was at the surface – I'd exploded back from the water into the air. For a while I couldn't think of anything, and I couldn't do anything except let out the old breath I'd been holding and take a couple of fresh, quick ones, and tread water – and hang on to that brick.

Pond water was trickiing down inside my nose and into my mouth, which I hate. But there was air all round and above, for me to breathe, to live.

And then I noticed they were shouting from the bank. They were cheering and shouting, 'Sausage! Sausage!' and the instructor was hallooing with his hands round his mouth, and bellowing to me: 'What on earth have you got there, Sausage?'

So then I turned myself properly round – I'd come up almost facing the fishermen at the other end of the Pond, but otherwise only a few feet from where I'd gone down; so that was all right. I turned round and swam to the bank and they hauled me out and gave me my glasses to have a good look at what I'd brought up from the bottom.

Because it wasn't a brick. It was just about the size and shape of one, but it was a tin – an old, old tin box with no paint left on it and all brown-black slime from the bottom of the Ponds. It was as heavy as a brick because it was full of mud. Don't get excited, as we did: there was nothing there but mud. We strained all the mud through our fingers, but there wasn't anything else there – not even a bit of old sandwich or the remains of bait. I thought there might have been, because the tin could have belonged to one of the old chaps that have always fished at the other end of the Ponds. They often bring their dinners with them in bags or tins, and they have tins for bait, too. It could have been dropped into the water at their end of the Ponds and got moved to our end with the movement of the water. Otherwise I don't know how that tin box can have got there. Anyway, it must have been there for years and years, by the look of it. When you think, it might have stayed there for years and years longer; perhaps stayed sunk under-water for ever.

I've cleaned the tin up and I keep it on the mantelpiece at home with my coin collection in it. I had to duck-dive later for another brick, and I got it all right, without being frightened at all; but it didn't seem to matter as much as coming up with the tin. I shall keep the tin as long as I live, and I might easily live to be a hundred.

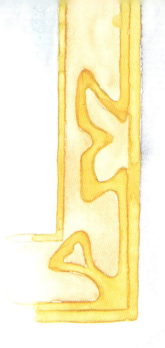

Philippa Pearce

TOOTHIE AND CAT

High on the hills above the city was a cave, well hidden away among the trees and the rocks and the bracken. And in that cave lived an old tramp with a gingery, greyish beard hanging to his waist, a greasy hat on his head, string tied just below the knees of his trousers, and one tooth that stuck out over his beard. Because of this he was known as Toothie, and he couldn't remember any other name. He couldn't remember very much at all, for his brain was as foggy as a November night. He was never bright even in his prime and he hadn't improved with the years. Nobody had ever cared for him much since his mother dumped him, wrapped in an old blanket, outside a police station, and then made off as fast as she could. Toothie tried to keep away from police stations ever after.

Below the hills in the city lived Cat, Cat the Black and the Bad, a streak of a cat with claws as sharp as daggers and a heart as black as his tatty fur. No one loved Cat. Once he was dropped in a river and left to drown. But you don't drown animals like Cat that easily. He got out, and survived, by hatred, mostly. He hated people and children and bright lights and kindness. He loved fighting and stealing, roof-tops and alleys and, most of all, dustbins. He relied on them when the birds grew careful, or too many kitchen doors were shut. In the day-time he thieved and slept on walls in patches of sunlight. At night he rampaged across roof-tops, wailing and caterwauling. So he lived for some years, till one morning he dropped from a roof-top a bit carelessly, and a car speeding

through the dawn grazed his leg. Snarling and swearing, he limped to the side of the road, where Toothie, who had also been raiding dustbins, found him. He was pleased, for he'd found a very meaty chicken carcase.

He walked all round Cat, who spat at him. Then he popped a bit of chicken into the complaining mouth, and Cat stopped spitting, and ate instead. Toothie popped him in his old bag, and went back to the cave, where he made some chicken soup and tied a big leaf round the injured leg. After a time Cat stopped spitting at him, for he'd grown to like Toothie's smell. His leg healed.

Cat did not return to the city. It was summer. He hunted and Toothie cooked: stews and soups in his iron pot, other tasty dishes baked in mud packed at the base of the fire. Long warm days passed by in the green wood and the dark cave. Sometimes Toothie would sing and Cat purr, both rusty noises. That autumn was beautiful, warm and golden, with more nuts than had been seen for years. Toothie and Cat were well fed and content.

Until the night the October wind arrived, blowing cold, stripping the leaves off the trees, and it brought with it the sound of cats singing in the city below. Cat stirred in his sleep and woke up. He left Toothie's warmth to sit in the mouth of the cave, listening. Yes, there, again, came the yowling of cats. Cat shivered. He looked once at the old man, asleep, and slipped out into the night.

A fortnight later he came back, hungry, limping, wet and exhausted, longing for Toothie's warm fire, Toothie's food, Toothie's smelly company. But the cave was empty. The iron pot hung forlornly by the burnt-out fire. Toothie had gone.

Cat sat and washed himself, which is what cats do when they don't know what to do next. Then he searched through the woods, crying his strange, wild call. There was no Toothie. Cat slew an unwary bird who would have done better to have migrated and, still hungry, set off for the city.

Through the streets he ran, sniffing, investigating, fighting, always searching for Toothie's fascinating smell, and one day, a week or so later, he arrived at the City Hospital and knew that his friend was inside.

31

Now Cat was much cleverer than Toothie, and he knew from the smell of the hospital that that was where people were ill, and his cat brain put illness and chicken together. He'd got to find some chicken.

He tried as many houses as he had paws before he finally crept into a gleaming, shiny bright kitchen, and there on the immaculate tiled surface lay a scrumptious chicken leg on a plate of crisp salad. The salad Cat ignored, he was not a lettuce-eater, but he seized the chicken and was just about to leap through the partially opened window when the owner appeared, screamed like a whistling kettle and spent the rest of the day feeling very ill indeed, and telling anyone who could be made to listen how a fiendish monster had appeared like a black demon in her sacred kitchen. Cat kept increasing in size till he reached the dimensions of a mini-tiger.

A while later, the mini-tiger sat outside the hospital door and waited, chicken portion gripped firmly in teeth. Going in at the front door didn't seem like a good idea – it looked too busy and important. Cat had never liked front doors, anyway. Back or side doors were for the likes of him. So he slunk round the corner till he came to a dark staircase that went up and up and on and on. Right at the top were dozens of dustbins. Cat purred through the chicken. He liked those dustbins, homely and friendly, they were.

Beyond them was a door with two little round glass panels. It opened in the middle and swung as someone walked through. And Cat slid in, keeping a very low profile. He ran, chicken in mouth and stomach almost on the floor, through rows of beds, and then into another ward with yet more beds. In the third a little boy lay in bed, bored. He sat up and cried:

'There's cat. It's got something in its mouth. Good ole puss cat. Come here.'

He wanted Cat a lot, but Cat ran on. But now that he was spotted, pandemonium broke loose.

'Catch that cat!'
'Stop him!'

'Get that filthy animal out of here!'

As fast as he could, Cat ran on. Patients shouted as nurses ran to grab him.

But nothing could stop Cat now. Like a rocket swooshing into space, Cat shot down the ward to find Toothie. He dodged trolleys, ran under beds, ran over beds, squeezed between legs, narrowly missed cleaners, tripped up nurses carrying vases of flowers or trays, scattering people right and left to reach the bed with the screens round it where Toothie lay dying.

He'd collapsed with pneumonia a week after Cat had left him and somehow, shivering, coughing, full of pains, he'd crawled to the road, where a bus driver had driven him straight to the hospital despite complaints from some of the passengers. And since then, Toothie had lain in terror of the bright lights, the uniforms, the smells and the sounds, all too much for his mazed mind. He wanted to die.

Sister's voice rang out loud and clear.

'Stop that beast! It's got germs!'

Hands grabbed at Cat, missing narrowly. He shot through the screens and the doctor and nurses beside Toothie and up on to the bed. There on the whiter than white, brighter than bright, snowy, frosty, bleached, purified, disinfected, sterilised, decontaminated pillow Cat laid the dusty, greasy, tooth-marked chicken leg, just beside Toothie's head.

Shouts were all about him now.

But Toothie's eyes opened and he saw Cat. A triumphant burst of purring sounded through the ward. Come what might, Cat had arrived. He'd found Toothie.

Gene Kemp

SAVIOURS OF THE TRAIN

The Russian gentleman was so delighted with the strawberries that the three racked their brains to find some other surprise for him. But all the racking did not bring out any idea more novel than wild cherries. And this idea occurred to them next morning. They had seen the blossom on the trees in the spring, and they knew where to look for wild cherries now that cherry time was here. The trees grew all up and along the rocky face of the cliff out of which the mouth of the tunnel opened. There were all sorts of trees there, birches and beeches and baby oaks and hazels, and among them the cherry blossom had shone like snow and silver.

The mouth of the tunnel was some way from Three Chimneys, so Mother let them take their lunch with them in a basket. And the basket would do to bring the cherries back if they found any. She also lent them her silver watch so that they should not be late for tea. Peter's Waterbury had taken it into its head not to go since the day when Peter dropped it into the water-butt. And they started. When they got to the top of the cutting, they leaned over the fence and looked down to where the railway lines lay at the bottom of what, as Phyllis said, was exactly like a mountain gorge.

'If it wasn't for the railway at the bottom, it would be as though the foot of man had never been there, wouldn't it?'

The sides of the cutting were of grey stone, very roughly hewn. Indeed, the top part of the cutting had been a little natural glen that had been cut deeper to bring it down to the level of the tunnel's mouth. Among the rocks, grass and flowers grew, and seeds dropped by birds in the crannies of the stone had taken root and grown into bushes and trees that overhung the cutting. Near the tunnel was a flight of steps leading down to the line – just wooden

bars roughly fixed into the earth – a very steep and narrow way, more like a ladder than a stair.

'We'd better get down,' said Peter; 'I'm sure the cherries would be quite easy to get at from the side of the steps. You remember it was there we picked the cherry blossoms that we put on the rabbit's grave.'

So they went along the fence towards the little swing gate that is at the top of these steps. And they were almost at the gate when Bobbie said:

'Hush. Stop! What's that?'

'That' was a very odd noise indeed – a soft noise, but quite plainly to be heard through the sound of the wind in the branches, and the hum and whir of the telegraph wires. It was a sort of rustling, whispering sound. As they listened it stopped and then it began again.

And this time it did not stop, but it grew louder and more rustling and rumbling.

'Look' – cried Peter, suddenly – 'the tree over there!'

The tree he pointed at was one of those that have rough grey leaves and white flowers. The berries, when they come, are bright scarlet, but if you pick them, they disappoint you by turning black before you get them home. And, as Peter pointed, the tree was moving – not just the way trees ought to move when the wind blows through them, but all in one piece, as though it were a live creature and were walking down the side of the cutting.

'It's moving!' cried Bobbie. 'Oh, look! and so are the others. It's like the woods in *Macbeth*.'

'It's magic,' said Phyllis, breathlessly. 'I always knew the railway was enchanted.'

It really did seem a little like magic. For all the trees for about twenty yards of the opposite bank seemed to be slowly walking down towards the railway line, the tree with the grey leaves bringing up the rear like some old shepherd driving a flock of green sheep.

'What is it? Oh, what is it?' said Phyllis; 'it's much too magic for me. I don't like it. Let's go home.'

But Bobbie and Peter clung fast to the rail and watched breathlessly. And Phyllis made no movement towards going home by herself.

The trees moved on and on. Some stones and loose earth fell down and rattled on the railway metals far below.

'It's *all* coming down,' Peter tried to say, but he found there was hardly any voice to say it with. And, indeed, just as he spoke, the great rock, on the top of which the walking trees were, leaned slowly forward. The trees, ceasing to walk, stood still and shivered. Leaning with the rock, they seemed to hesitate a moment, and then rock and trees and grass and bushes, with a rushing sound, slipped right away from the face of the cutting and fell on the line with a blundering crash that could have been heard half a mile off. A cloud of dust rose up.

'Oh,' said Peter, in awestruck tones, 'isn't it exactly like when coals come in? – if there wasn't any roof to the cellar and you could see down.'

'Look what a great mound it's made!' said Bobbie.

'Yes, it's right across the down line,' said Phyllis.

'That'll take some sweeping up,' said Bobbie.

'Yes,' said Peter slowly. He was still leaning on the fence.

'Yes,' he said again, still more slowly.

Then he stood upright.

'The 11.29 down hasn't gone by yet. We must let them know at the station, or there'll be a most frightful accident.'

'Let's run,' said Bobbie, and began.

But Peter cried, 'Come back!' and looked at Mother's watch. He was very prompt and businesslike and his face looked whiter than they had ever seen it.

'No time,' he said; 'it's ten miles away, and it's past eleven.'

'Couldn't we,' suggested Phyllis, breathlessly, 'couldn't we climb up a telegraph post and do something to the wires?'

'We don't know how,' said Peter.

'They do it in war,' said Phyllis; 'I know I've heard of it.'

'They only *cut* them, silly,' said Peter, 'and that doesn't do any good. And we couldn't cut them even if we got up, and we couldn't get up. If we had anything red, we could go down on the line and wave it.'

'But the train wouldn't see us till it got round the corner, and then it could see the mound just as well as us,' said Phyllis; 'better, because it's much bigger than us.'

'If we only had something red,' Peter repeated, 'we could go round the corner and wave to the train.'

'We might wave anyway.'

'They'd only think it was just *us*, as usual. We've waved so often before. Anyway, let's get down.'

They got down the steep stairs. Bobbie was pale and shivering. Peter's face looked thinner than usual. Phyllis was red-faced and damp with anxiety.

'Oh, how hot I am!' she said; 'and I thought it was going to be cold; I wish we hadn't put on our –' she stopped short, and then ended in quite a different tone – 'our flannel petticoats.'

Bobbie turned at the bottom of the stairs.

'Oh, yes,' she cried, '*they're* red! Let's take them off.'

They did, and with the petticoats rolled up under their arms, ran along the railway, skirting the newly fallen mound of stones and rock and earth, and bent, crushed, twisted trees. They ran at their best pace. Peter led, but the girls were not far behind. They reached the corner that hid the mound from the straight line of railway that ran half a mile without curve or corner.

'Now,' said Peter, taking hold of the largest flannel petticoat.

'You're not' – Phyllis faltered – 'you're not going to *tear* them?'

'Shut up,' said Peter, with brief sternness.

'Oh, yes,' said Bobbie, 'tear them into little bits if you like. Don't you see, Phil, if we can't stop the train, there'll be a real live accident, with people *killed*. Oh, horrible! Here, Peter, you'll never tear it through the band.'

She took the red flannel petticoat from him and tore it off an inch from the band. Then she tore the other in the same way.

'There!' said Peter, tearing in his turn. He divided each petticoat

37

into three pieces. 'Now, we've got six flags.' He looked at the watch again. 'And we've got seven minutes. We must have flagstaffs.'

The knives given to boys are, for some odd reason, seldom of the kind of steel that keeps sharp. The young saplings had to be broken off. Two came up by the roots. The leaves were stripped from them.

'We must cut holes in the flags, and run the sticks through the holes,' said Peter. And the holes were cut. The knife was sharp enough to cut flannel with. Two of the flags were set up in heaps of loose stones beneath the sleepers of the down line. Then Phyllis and Roberta took each a flag, and stood ready to wave it as soon as the train came in sight.

'I shall have the other two myself,' said Peter, 'because it was my idea to wave something red.'

'They're our petticoats, though,' Phyllis was beginning, but Bobbie interrupted –

'Oh, what does it matter who waves what, if we can only save the train?'

Perhaps Peter had not rightly calculated the number of minutes it would take the 11.29 to get from the station to the place where they were, or perhaps the train was late. Anyway, it seemed a very long time that they waited.

Phyllis grew impatient. 'I expect the watch is wrong and the train's gone by,' said she.

Peter relaxed the heroic attitude he had chosen to show off his two flags. And Bobbie began to feel sick with suspense.

It seemed to her that they had been standing there for hours and hours, holding those silly little red flannel flags that no one would ever notice. The train wouldn't care. It would go rushing by them and tear round the corner and go crashing into that awful mound. And everyone would be killed. Her hands grew very cold and trembled so that she could hardly hold the flag. And then came the distant rumble and hum of the metals, and a puff of white steam showed far away along the stretch of line.

'Stand firm,' said Peter, 'and wave like mad. When it gets to that big furze bush step back, but go on waving! Don't stand *on* the line, Bobbie!'

The train came rattling along very, very fast.

'They don't see us! They won't see us! It's all no good!' cried Bobbie.

The two little flags on the line swayed as the nearing train shook and loosened the heaps of loose stones that held them up. One of them slowly leaned over and fell on the line. Bobbie jumped forward and caught it up, and waved it; her hands did not tremble now.

It seemed that the train came on as fast as ever. It was very near now.

'Keep off the line, you silly cuckoo!' said Peter, fiercely.

'It's no good,' Bobbie said again.

'Stand back!' cried Peter, suddenly, and he dragged Phyllis back by the arm.

But Bobbie cried, 'Not yet, not yet!' and waved her two flags right over the line. The front of the engine looked black and enormous. Its voice was loud and harsh.

'Oh, stop, stop, stop!' cried Bobbie. No one heard her. At least Peter and Phyllis didn't, for the oncoming rush of the train covered the sound of her voice with a mountain of sound. But afterwards she used to wonder whether the engine itself had not heard her. It seemed almost as though it had – for it slackened swiftly, slackened and stopped, not twenty yards from the place where Bobbie's two flags waved over the line. She saw the great black engine stop dead, but somehow she could not stop waving the flags. And when the driver and the fireman had got off the engine and Peter and Phyllis had gone to meet them and pour out their excited tale of the awful mound just round the corner, Bobbie still waved the flags but more and more feebly and jerkily.

Edith Nesbit
an extract from
The Railway Children

Culford Books wish to thank the following for their kind permission to use their material:

'Down River' Richard Church an extract from THE CAVE William Heinemann Limited © the Estate of Richard Church. 'The Giant and the Mite' Eleanor Farjeon from THE LITTLE BOOKROOM New Oxford Library. 'Arap Sang and the Cranes' Humphrey Harman from TALES TOLD NEAR A CROCODILE Hutchinson. 'Toothie and Cat' Gene Kemp from DOG DAYS AND CAT NAPS Faber and Faber. 'Uninvited Ghosts' Penelope Lively from FRANK AND POLLY MUIR'S BIG DIPPER William Heinemann Limited. Text © Penelope Lively 1981. Reprinted by permission of William Heinemann Limited. 'Return to Air' Philippa Pearce from WHAT THE NEIGHBOURS DID Longman Young Books 1972. Copyright © 1959, 1967, 1969, 1972 by Philippa Pearce. 'How Loki Outwitted a Giant' Barbara Leonie Picard from HAMISH HAMILTON BOOK OF GIANTS selected by William Mayne. Hamish Hamilton.

This collection of short stories © Jennifer Wilson 1989
Introduction © Jennifer Wilson 1989
Illustrations © Graham Cooper 1989
TELL TALES © Culford Books 1989

First published in Great Britain in 1989 by
Blackie & Son Ltd
All rights reserved

Conceived, edited, designed and produced by Culford Books,
Sunningwell House, Sunningwell, Abingdon,
Oxfordshire OX13 6RD
House Editor Penelope Miller
Designed by Judith Allan
Photoset by Burgess & Son (Abingdon) Ltd

British Library Cataloguing in Publication Data

Tell Tales.
  Vol. 2
  I. Wilson, Jennifer II. Cooper, Graham
  398.2'1

  ISBN 0-216-92732-3

Blackie & Son Ltd
7 Leicester Place
London WC2H 7BP

Printed and bound in Great Britain by
Purnell Book Production Ltd